SHIPWRECKS
OF IRELAND

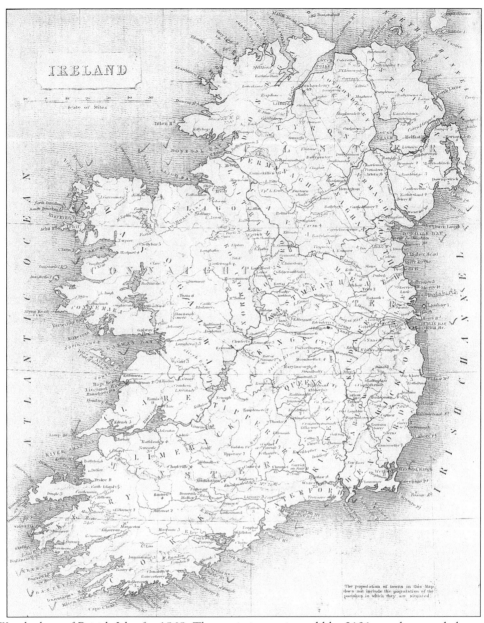

Wreck chart of British Isles for 1868. The statistics are incredible: 2131 wrecks recorded, total losses were 629 and 824 lives lost. The number of vessels at sea was, however, enormous with some 100,000 sailing ships in the coastal trade.

SHIPWRECKS OF IRELAND

Edward J. Bourke

TEMPUS

First published 2000
Copyright © Edward J. Bourke, 2000

Tempus Publishing Limited
The Mill, Brimscombe Port,
Stroud, Gloucestershire, GL5 2QG

ISBN 0 7524 1764 9

Typesetting and origination by
Tempus Publishing Limited
Printed in Great Britain by
Midway Clark Printing, Wiltshire

Lofs of the Prince of Wales Packet

The troopship *Rochdale* was wrecked at the Martello Tower, at Seapoint, on 18 September 1807. Another ship of the same convoy, the *Prince of Wales*, was wrecked at Blackrock House nearby. They had sailed from the Pigeon House harbour in Dublin with the 9th West Kent Regiment bound for the continent. Some 100 men, women and children were lost on the *Prince of Wales* and 265 on the *Rochdale*.

Contents

Introduction

The coast of Ireland has seen gales smash Armada galleons, ruthless torpedo attacks on shipping, fog blinded liners crash into cliffs and hundreds of small coasters founder. I estimate that there have been some 12,000 wrecks on the Irish coast. Many were never named and significant numbers were not recorded in official records. Often the sad account states that wreckage from an unknown ship was washed ashore or even that wreckage was seen at the foot of steep cliffs. My conclusion is that the Lloyds List includes only thirty per cent of Irish coast wrecks in the period to 1820. There are few reports from the West of Ireland, primarily because of light shipping traffic, but also because of lack of an agent and active shipping traffic with England. The reporting from remote areas of the West coast must therefore be presumed to be almost non-existent. In the absence of newspaper accounts no information remains. The loss of a ship was often ambiguous as an insurance total loss might be restored, or a vessel which reached safety could be scrapped as a constructive total loss. Photographs and illustrations of shipwrecks are even more rare and few have survived. Two of the finest collections were made by Mr Ensor for his salvage work and Mr Jacob, the Lloyds agent at Waterford. Many individuals kept photographs from their own locality and these form a significant part of this book. Though several collections of old photographs have been assembled over the years, there is little of maritime interest and rarely material on shipwrecks.

The inclusion of some older images from etchings and illustrated magazines shows a particular style of shipwreck art which was popular at the time. Some of the photos come from postcards; sometimes there was sufficient interest in the shipwreck to justify the commercial production of a card. Some of these cards were sold on excursion boats out of Cork Harbour to allow the public see the wreck of the *Falls of Garry* and the stranded liner *Merrion*.

Some of the images are of poor quality, but the reader will appreciate that they may have been taken from a spray spattered headland during a storm, or even from an aircraft buffeted by the winds which put the ship in danger. Some have been retrieved from damaged prints.

The photographs found in this book are organised in a clockwise direction around the coast, with separate chapters covering rescue, wartime, artefacts and salvage.

THE NORTH EAST

The area around Belfast came to commercial prominence quite late in the Industrial Revolution. The main port was Strangford, an unusual location for a port because of the treacherous current, whirlpool and dangerous rocks at the harbour mouth. It only fell into decline when a decision was taken not to extend the railway to the port. Belfast began to dominate from the 1800s onwards. The wide natural harbour there is much more easily approached, and the only obstructions to shipping are the Copeland islands near the Bangor shore.

EAST COAST

The eastern seaboard of Ireland is the busiest for commercial shipping, primarily because of the connections with Britain. Chester and Hoylake were important ferry ports until the eighteenth century, but then the sands of Dee choked the river. The shipping traffic then moved to Liverpool and Holyhead. As a result of Captain Bligh's survey and recommendations, the Dublin port commenced the construction of the retaining walls. The building of the North and South Bull walls at Dublin washed away the bar and enabled shipping to cross the shallows which had blocked the port entrance. The bar and North Bull bank caused the loss of many vessels. It is estimated that Dublin Bay must have had some 1,000 shipwrecks from the earliest times to the present day.

In an easterly gale, ship rash enough to set sail from Liverpool were wrecked on the Irish coast in great numbers. The sandbanks stretching from the Burford Bank outside Dublin run in a line the whole way to Wexford. The succession of names, Kish, Codling, India, Arklow,

Blackwater, Moneyweights, and Barham strike fear into the hearts of mariners even today. The ability of some of the banks to move with currents is not just a tall tale. The largest ship ever stranded on the banks was the car transporter *Asian Parade*, caught on the Codling Bank on 6 February 2000. She had a lucky escape and was towed off with only light damage after her oil was removed to lighten the ship and prevent pollution.

SOUTH EAST

The corner of Ireland occupied by the two counties of Wexford and Waterford has a great seafaring tradition. The Waterford to Newfoundland trade was most extensive. Wexford maintains several fishing fleets and the harbour of Rosslare became a prominent ferry port once a harbour was developed along with the railway. The coast is well-lit today, but the Hook light alone lit the coast from the earliest times. Many vessels were lost among the isolated rocks and banks when one lighthouse was obscured or mistaken for another. The sandy beach at Tramore was so frequently mistaken for Waterford harbour entrance that towers were placed on the headlands at either side to help identify the coast precisely.

CORK

The port of Cork is second only to Dublin, and came to the fore when the Royal Navy moved its base from Kinsale after the attempted French landing at Bantry Bay in 1796. The Kinsale fleet base served the West Indies traffic and was the place of assembly and dispersal for the convoys during various French Wars. The long rocky West Cork coast was the first landfall after a transatlantic voyage. The lack of modern navigation aids enjoyed today led many ships to crash into the remorseless cliffs in fog or snow. Cork Harbour, Cobh and Bantry Bay were fleet bases during the First World War and their importance to the Royal Navy was such that they and their protective artillery forts were only handed back to the Irish Government in 1938, some sixteen years after Independence in the rest of Ireland. Cork was the port of call for transatlantic liners and several were wrecked or had narrow escapes near the harbour mouth.

WEST COAST

The West Coast was always commercially deprived and suffered horribly during the Famine of 1845-1847. However, because of remoteness and poor roads, small coaster trading survived well into recent years. Trade tended to focus on Glasgow, and there were regular ferry services to cater for the seasonal emigration trade. Wrecks are scarce mainly because of light traffic. The wild Atlantic northern approaches and the coastline present the same threat to transatlantic shipping as the south. The most prominent harbour is Derry. It was from here that the Battle of the Atlantic was fought at the front line, rather than from Glasgow. The treaty port of Lough Swilly, which had been so vital in the First World War, was handed back in 1938 and the main base became Lisahally in the river Foyle. Because of the escort cover and aircover from Eglinton, Castle Archdale and Ballykelly, ships took the better covered northern approaches to the British ports. This also allowed them avoid hostile German aircraft based in France. During the Second World War the shipping attacks near Ireland tended to be off the Donegal coast.

RESCUE

No less than three lifeboats were lost during rescues around Ireland. The first was the Dublin Port Sandycove lifeboat in 1836. The Dun Laoghaire or Kingstown boat was lost in 1896 and the Fethard-on-Sea boat in 1915. Gallantry at sea was not restricted to lifeboat crews. The coastguards and their rowing boats saved hundreds from shipwrecks. By far the most important service performed from the coastguard barracks were the rocket rescues. Lines were fired into the rigging of ships and lines drawn out to the distressed vessel. The crew were saved using a breeches buoy. The rescue attempt by Captain Boyd and his sailors from the HMS *Ajax* in Kingstown was a classic of its kind, but ended tragically for both rescuers and rescued. Lighthouse men and lightship crews were well placed near hazards to shipping and performed several rescues when shipwrecks occurred close to their station. Helicopter rescues took over in recent years and the crews performed equal miracles. They too had their accidents, like the Dauphin helicopter crash at Tramore with the loss of four Irish Air Corps crew. A Dragonfly helicopter of the Fleet Air Arm narrowly escaped disaster when it crashed at Narin, Co. Donegal, during the rescue of the Greenhaven crew.

Modern rescue services based on helicopters and lifeboats are a far cry from the situation in former times. An interesting insight is given in the Board of Trade return for 1913-1914. It records that in that year 115 were rescued from shipwreck by rocket apparatus, 135 by lifeboats, 81 by coastguard boats, 682 by passing vessels and 762 by their own ships' lifeboats. The role of passing vessels is noteworthy, as marine traffic was dense in contrast to that of today.

FIRST WORLD WAR

The First World War was fought with great ferocity just off the coast of Ireland. Between 1914 and 1918 some 400 ships were sunk almost within sight of the Irish coast. Naval bases were initially ill-equipped to deal with the submarine menace, but as armed trawlers and the Flower class sloops came into the action there were fleets of vessels to combat the U-boats. Despite this array of force submarines were able to penetrate the barrages at Rathlin and Tuskar to enter the Irish Sea right until the end of the war. Roy Stokes has documented some forty submarine forays into the Irish Sea right up until the sinking of the *Leinster* six weeks before the Armistice. The set of photographs involving the Flower class sloops off West Cork is particularly remarkable. They helped the rescue of the crew of the *Malmanger* on 12 March, and a few days later on 17 March the *Mignonette* was sunk. The next day the *Alyssum* was mined and sank. Submarine attacks were so common off the Fastnet that a British submarine was stationed in the vicinity to hunt the hunters The *U 81* was torpedoed by *E 54* when the U-boat surfaced to read the name of a ship.

SALVAGE

The rescue of the crew was the first concern, but then attention turned to saving the ship and its cargo. The history of salvage in Ireland is associated with many of the most famous names in diving, Jacob Johnson, Brathwaite, Deane, Spalding, Gann and Damant. There were prominent engineers as well – even Brunel came to look at the *Great Britain*. The most important salvage firms were: the Liverpool and Glasgow Salvage association, McCauslands of Portaferry, Smit Tak, Riesdon Beazley, Ensor and Palmers of Queenstown. Often, when victory was almost in their grasp, the seas rose-up and reclaimed the wreck.

Early times

The fury with which primitive communities descended upon a stricken vessel can only be regarded with a sense of awe. Tales abound of the ferocity of wreckers and their cruel deeds. Many tales are related which must be apocryphal. Foremost among these is the story of the light tied to a cow's horns, a horse's tail or even carried by men to give the impression of the lantern of a ship rising and falling at anchor. Another story is of a raft or shallow draught vessel with a lantern luring a ship over a reef in darkness. False beacons on shore could be used to lure a ship into a landlocked bay if the keepers of the true light were intoxicated and their beacon extinguished. The most horrific tales involve the slaughter of survivors and the pillage of their jewellery. There is some explanation for these tales and traditions in the bizarre regulations which applied in less civilised ages.

In the third century BC the peoples of the Mediterranean had the Rhodian code which survived 1,000 years until the Crusades. Then the assizes of Jerusalem took over. The Tabula Amalfitana were established in the tenth century on the island of Amalfi, and covered wreckage among other maritime matters. On the Eastern Mediterranean the Byzantine authorities had the code of maritime law known as Basilika. Under Brehon Law in Ireland, when a ship was wrecked its cargo belonged to the people of the locality of the wreck. It is not surprising that this convenient state of affairs was little more than *laissez-faire*.

Common Law

Ancient common law directed that the cargo of a wrecked ship belonged to the king, who might assign his rights to a favoured noble or landowner. For instance in 1174 the abbot of Buildwas in Shropshire was granted the rights of St Mary's abbey in Dublin by Henry II 'to include all the shipwrecks that might happen on their land'. In 1684 the rich rights to wreck on the South Bull were disputed between the Dublin Corporation and the Admiralty. Later, in 1728, the City of Dublin observed that 'Captain Vernon assumes the right of the City by taking upon him the right to seize such things that are cast on the shore at Clontarf by shipwreck which is the undoubted right of the city of Dublin.'

Monarchs before Henry I had complete possession of wrecked property. Towards the end of his reign Henry I decreed that wrecked goods should not be considered lost to the owner or become the crown property if there were survivors.

Henry II expanded this situation in 1120, decreeing that if any man or beast survived a shipwreck, the cargo would not be deemed wreck and the goods would remain the property of the owner. This explains the strange observation in reports that mention some animal surviving the wreck and omit other significant details. This led to the allegation that sailors washed ashore were murdered so that the goods would be considered wreck. This state of affairs was further modified in 1236.

Richard I changed matters somewhat by stating that all persons escaping alive from a shipwreck should retain their goods. A wreck or wreckage should only be considered the property of the crown when neither an owner, nor heirs of a late owner could be found. Richard I is believed to have developed the Rolls of Oleron at a maritime court at the island of the same name near Bordeaux. There were thirty-seven articles, which, promulgated by Richard, formed a basis of maritime law for several centuries in European countries. The code provided that treacherous pilots who deliberately drove ships ashore should be hanged on gibbets. If a pilot colluded with lords of the manor who profited from their actions by having ships beached where they had right of salvage, the punishment was severe indeed. The lord was to be tied to a post in the middle of his own house and the house set on fire at the four corners. Prior to this dreadful fate his goods were to be forfeited and given to those injured. If this were not sufficient the ruins of the house were to be converted into a place for the sale of hogs and swine.

The penalty for murder of shipwrecked folk was to be plunged into the sea until half dead and then stoned to death. A milder sentence was provided for negligent pilots who were to have their goods seized to repair the loss. However if their goods were insufficient they were to be beheaded. Captains were advised that they should be persuaded that the man had not the means to make good the loss , before they cut off his head. The Rolls of Oleron were incorporated into The Laws of Wisbeg, The Judgements of Damme in Flanders and the Purple Book of Bruges.

The wrecking situation was so serious that in 1169 the Church found it necessary to take a stance. The Lateran council held at Rome condemned wrecking and exhibiting false signals.

In 1353 Edward III in ordained that four men would be appointed receivers and would try to find the rightful owner of wreckage. This is the first mention of receivers and the title applies to this day to the officers of customs warranted to administer wreck. In 1375 he gathered a solemn inquisition at Queensborough, consisting of eighteen of the most famous seafarers of the time. The Black Book of the Admiralty was commenced to record decisions on maritime law. The work was continued by Richard II and Henry IV.

George II produced a new act which set out its intentions. Despite the existing laws there had been many wicked deeds relating to shipwrecks. Thus he provided for penalties. Death was also prescribed for hanging out misleading lights to bring vessels into distress. Death was prescribed for the murder or prevention of the escape of shipwrecked persons and for stealing the goods whether there were survivors or not. Later laws reduced the penalties to imprisonment but penal servitude for life was the penalty for scuttling or burning a ship to defraud the insurance.

In the seventeenth century, Hugo Grotius, a Dutch lawyer, invented the concept of *mare liberum* which, as the name in Latin suggests, described the high seas as free. The concept was that outside territorial waters there was no territorial claim. Originally the limit of a country's jurisdiction was three miles, then reckoned to be the range of a cannon shot.

Research by Alan Roddie revealed the grant of salvage rights on the Irish Coast to several individuals, although particular wrecks are not specified. The Kings Warrant Book of 12 December 1694 records that Lt-Col. Edward Pierce was granted rights to all salvage within fifty leagues of the

Staggs of Broadhaven until 1702, provided he 'keep a faithful account and bring any recovered goods to London'. Similarly on 21 May 1705 John Knap, Samuel Cope and William Rayner petitioned to be granted wrecks on the west coast of Ireland for fourteen years. An Andrew Becker was given a warrant on 22 December 1715 to fish for wrecks in America and Ireland.

Disputes

The case of the Danish East Indiaman *Golden Lion*, wrecked at Ballyheigue, led to protracted battles between the Danish and British authorities. The Danes claimed that she was beached not wrecked. The Crosbie family and other locals felt that they were deprived of their salvage due and robbed the entire load of silver. Arthur Crosbie was tried in Dublin and acquitted. A proclamation was issued by the Lord Lieutenant on 13 March 1731 looking for the twelve chests of silver and the robbers. Two cases are mentioned in official papers. They were *Rosina* in 1825 and the *Thomas & Jane* at Liscannor in 1822. The number of shipwrecks in the early part of the nineteenth century led to the Merchant Shipping Act of 1854. The Act described categories of wreck as jetsam, flotsam and laggan (material buoyed to be recovered later). It provided that the receiver could summon men and sailors to assist and also impress carts or equipment to save goods. It provided that anyone who provided a service to save life or goods was entitled to reward by the ship owners. Penalties were clearly laid out for plundering wreck and failing to report salvaged goods to the receiver. However, locals in coastal areas still regarded wreckage as their own. Even as late as the end of the last century there were pitched battles between coastguards and wreckers where militia had to be called in to fight mobs on the seashore. Such an incident occurred at the wreck of the *Chicago* in Cork in 1868. An enquiry was held into the wreck of the *San Francisco* at Clonakilty on 7 January 1867. The local landlord was Mr Beamish and his role in the matter was complicated to say the least. Coastguards fired at the mob which assembled.

One of the last claims of rights of Lord of the Manor occurred in Ireland in 1928. The SS *Garthloch* of Stockton foundered off Cahore, Co. Wexford in March 1928 and flour was washed ashore. The insurers, Lloyds, abandoned their interest and the owners of the land at the George estate claimed salvage rights. The claim was made but as the value was not considerable it was not pursued. The basis was that a patent had been awarded on 26 February in the tenth year of the reign of William III to Joost Earl of Albermarle which had been conveyed on 19 March 1703. This allowed all rights and easements including wreck and over all rights of the sea. The stretch of coast covered was between Ballymonisbeg and Ballinoulart. A group of English divers claimed to be salvors in possession of the three 1588 Armada wrecks at Streedagh in the early 1990s. Their claim was disputed by the Irish State in a protracted series of cases.

Modern Developments

The UN Law of the Sea convention, led to the Merchant Shipping Salvage and Wreck Act of 1994 and radically changed the situation in Ireland. It forbids the boarding of any wreck without the permission of the master or owner. The status of salvor in possession is therefore altered. Especially in the case of pollution the State is given extensive powers.

The National Monuments Amendment Act (No.17 of 1987) vests control of any wreck over 100 years old in the Irish State and also allows for the application of a Heritage Order to any more modern wreck of historical importance. Such an order has been applied to the *Lusitania* and its effect is to create an exclusion zone for diving in a wide area in the vicinity. Permits to dive must be obtained even by the owner of the wreck.

Admiralty law took a new twist in 1989 when the *Central America* case was judged in Norfolk Virginia. The Columbus America group was granted possession of a wrecked ship 160 miles offshore. The American court, with Judge Calvitt Clarke presiding, also heard a case between two Americans, Beamis and Gentile, where Beamis's ownership of the wreck was disputed by a company Fifty Fathoms Ventures. The Norfolk court found that it did have jurisdiction since the admiralty jurisdiction of the US is not limited by the seas involved whether within the Irish twelve mile limit or not.

Now an International Maritime court has been established at Hamburg under the auspices of the United Nations. One hundred and six states have signed the convention. The European Union has signed as an entity but has not ratified. It is expected that Britain and the USA may sign up in the future. This finalises work commenced by the League of Nations in the 1930s.

One

North East

The *Davaar* went aground at Briggs Reef on 7 July 1895. The steamer was refloated, but while working to free the wreck, the tug *Ranger* of the Liverpool and Glasgow Salvage Association struck the wreck of the *Emily* and sank.

The Fleetwood trawler *Shakleton* was wrecked at Grennan Bo on the north side of Rathlin on 1 March 1930. The crew were rescued from the bottom of 200-foot cliffs by the Rathlin rescue team. The *Shakleton* was built in 1913 at Selby. She was returning from fishing grounds at St Kilda.

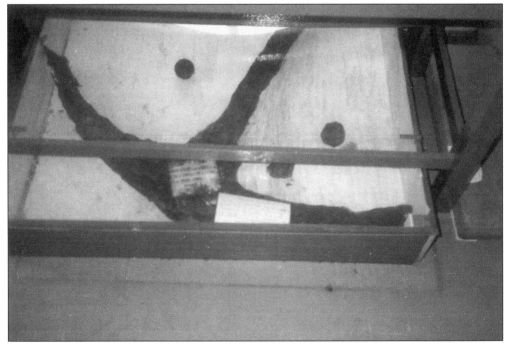

An *Armada* anchor was found by coastguards near Rutland Island in 1890. It was displayed outside the United Services Club at Pall Mall in London and then in the Franciscan Museum at Rossinolough.

The Dublin motor vessel *Liveox*, ashore at Ballyfrench Bay.

The liner *Letitia* went ashore between Groomsport and Orlock in August 1935 during fog. After a struggle the vessel was floated off.

Vinthfjord went ashore en route from Peel to Portavogie. She was refloated from McCammon rocks, Portavogie in May 1973 and hulked at the Isle of Man.

The 835-ton Liverpool & Glasgow Salvage Association vessel *Ranger*, built as gunboat for the RN in 1881, purchased in 1892 and scrapped in 1953. In 1968 the LGSA group withdrew from salvage due to lack of business and concentrated on survey of ships and cargoes.

The *Ulrica* was wrecked at the old lighthouse island on the Copeland Islands on 7 January 1897. She was built at Barclay Curles on the Clyde in 1884.

Mc Causland divers working on the wreck of the *Mary Anne* at Strangford, *c.*1900.

The 6,538 ton cable steamer *Anglia*, struck the west side of Ballyquentin point on 15 December 1906. Though seriously damaged, she was refloated on 27 April 1907.

William Bailey ashore at the Mast port, Tara Point, Co. Down, 17 August 1902 . The cargo of cotton and tallow was unloaded and the ship was refloated by McCauslands of Portaferry.

Anna Catherina aground at Kearney point on 5 April 1977. The captain was thought to have mistaken Portpatrick for Portaferry and ran onto Kearney point. Initially, she managed to reverse clear but grounded a second time. Luckily she was towed off the next day and resumed her voyage to Sweden. The South Rock light was changed from white to red to avoid confusion with Killintringan light.

The *Frida Blokzul* went ashore at Kearney point on 6 March 1962 and was refloated.

The *Lochgarry* sank on 21 January 1942 a mile off Rue Point on Rathlin Island. The ex-MacBrayne ferry was bound from Glasgow to Oban to embark troops for the Faroes. She strayed across the channel in a storm and sank after striking Torr Rock. Most escaped but twenty-six were lost when a lifeboat struck a rock and sank. The propeller was salvaged in April 1973.

The destroyer HMS *Mystic* and the *Oriania* went aground at Torr head during the First World War along with several more ships. An outbound convoy from Liverpool lost its bearings in fog. The intention was to pass between Rathlin and the British coast. Four steamers and a destroyer went ashore and were lying parallel under Torr Head when the fog lifted. Two further merchantmen went ashore on Rathlin. A rescue tug, HMS *Sonia*, and a destroyer pulled all the ships off without serious damage. The exact date is not known. A similar incident happened at Ballyquentin on 21 January 1942.

The 14,000-ton heavy cruiser HMS *Drake* sank at Church Bay on Rathlin on 2 October 1916. She was part of the escort for a convoy when she was torpedoed by *U 79*. She anchored in Church Bay but sank just as the destroyer *Martin* took off her crew. The *Mendip Range* collided with the *Drake* as she raced for shallow water and had to be beached to avoid sinking. The convoy meantime milled about Rathlin Sound in confusion and the *Lugano* became a second victim of *U 79*.

On 20 July 1940 the tramp steamer *Troutpool* was at anchor a mile off Bangor. She had come into Belfast for degaussing protection from magnetic mines. The engines were restarted and she was swung for compass adjustment, but she was immediately struck by one mine and minutes later, by a second. Eleven crewmen were killed and she sank in seven fathoms. Acoustic mines laid by German aircraft the night before were presumed to be responsible.

The Schooner JMK was wrecked at Bangor on 26 November 1905

On 22 September 1846, the *Great Britain* left Liverpool for New York with 180 passengers. The newly established light at St John's point apparently caused confusion, as the ship's chart had not been updated since May when the light was lit.

The *Great Britain* was protected from winter gales by a flexible breakwater of wattles designed by Brunel himself.

The *Great Britain* was released from the rocks which had penetrated the hull by levering the whole ship up 20 feet onto a platform to allow navvies to chip away the boulders.

THE BOWS OF THE "GREAT BRITAIN."

On 27 August 1847 the *Great Britain* was towed off. The accident bankrupted the Great Western Steamship Company. The salvage alone had cost £22,000, on top of a cost overrun on the building of about £50,000. In addition, despite a huge publicity campaign, she failed to attract sufficient passengers. After a period tied up, the ship was sold and refitted for the Australian emigrant trade which she served for some twenty years until her A1 passenger certificate was withdrawn by Lloyds. Then she spent a time in the coal trade before being abandoned at Port Stanley as a hulk. The *Great Britain* was recovered from the Falkland Islands in 1970 and carried to Bristol on a barge. She is undergoing preservation in the very dock where she was built.

The liberty ship *Georgetown Victory* was wrecked at Killard point on 30 April 1946. The 1400 demobbed sailors and marines aboard escaped before the ship broke in two.

Two

East

The *Irish Trader* was wrecked at Baltray on 2 February 1974. She carried fertiliser bound for Drogheda. The sand at Baltray beach is unusually soft and vehicles could not approach the wreck to lighten her. The ship sank rapidly into the sand and remains there to this day.

The *Tayleur* was built especially for the Australian emigrant trade. The Kalgoorlie gold rush caused unprecedented demand for passages to Australia and a crash building programme sought to satisfy the need for ships. The *Tayleur* was the largest iron sailing ship on the UK register at the time. Just like the *Titanic* she was on her maiden voyage for the White Star Line with emigrants when she was wrecked on Lambay on 28 January 1854. Some 360 aboard were lost.

The *Tayleur* sailing notice advertised her impending departure for Melbourne on 17 January and boasted of her size and speed. Only the sail and steamer *Great Britain* and the American sailing ships *Comet* and *Himalaya* were larger.

A memorial card to victims of the *Tayleur* disaster. Curiously neither name appears on the list of victims published in the *Liverpool Mercury*. The Warrington newspaper said that 660 were aboard, others say 580. Some 640 names have been traced using a combination of Dublin, Liverpool, Belfast and Limerick papers. Since 288 survived, the total number lost must therefore be about 370 persons.

The *Tayleur* was salvaged by the Dublin firm Shannon's and considerable material was recovered. The wreck auction was held on 8 June 1854. No account of Shannon's or the auction has survived.

Illustrated London News artists' impression of the wrecked *Tayleur*.

A headstone from the cargo, the binnacle and a toilet from the *Tayleur* held at Newbridge House, Donabate.

Among the cargo of the *Tayleur* was a huge quantity of willow pattern plates and crockery. Curiously, nearly all were faulty seconds which had been in storage for some years. The new inhabitants of the Australian goldrush towns were less fussy than English buyers. The dates attributed to the pottery marks were all around 1844, nearly ten years earlier than the wreck. Some say that the pottery was held unsold in a store, but others maintain that the marks were pattern marks.

The Tayleur Fund was used to assist the survivors and the dependants of the victims. The fund then awarded medals for gallant rescues in the Dublin area for the next sixty years. The fund continued until 1913, when the remaining £1,500 was used for the provision of a petrol-engined Dun Laoghaire lifeboat for the RNLI.

The paddle steamer *Queen Victoria* sank off the Bailey lighthouse in Dublin Bay on 14 February 1853 with the loss of eighty of the 120 aboard. The 337-ton ship was built for the City of Dublin Steam Packet Company in 1837. She struck the rocks just under the lighthouse in a snowstorm.

Figurehead from the *Queen Victoria*. The face was badly damaged but restored at the Maritime Museum using a Victorian penny as a model.

The *Scarlet Buccaneer* was wrecked on Howth Pier on 16 November 1995. One crewman was lost when the trawler lost power approaching the harbour.

Sailing trawler typical of Dublin Bay smacks, abandoned at Sutton.

The *Antelope* was one of the last sailing schooners trading around Ireland. She contained components of an earlier American vessel wrecked on the Saltees in around 1885. She ended her days on the beach at Bull Island, Dollymount on 13 December 1950. The island formed as a result of building the North or Bull Wall which prevented the sand from encroaching into the port channel. More than a hundred vessels met their fate in this area when they missed the entrance to Dublin port.

In 1891 the *Wanderer* was dismasted on her maiden voyage and towed into Kingstown. She grounded on the Burford bank on her way out, and was assisted by the tug *Wrestler* of Liverpool. The *Wanderer* is the subject of a book and a poem by John Masefield.

The Dublin Port tugs *Colliemore* and *Ben Eadar* succeeded in saving the 818 ton collier *Kylemore* of Liverpool on 21 January 1956. The mailboat *Cambria* answered a distress message when broadcast, but resumed her journey when the *Slieve Bloom* relieved her. Wicklow lifeboat also attended. She had developed a list some 20 miles south of the Bailey lighthouse during a force 8 gale. The *Citric* foundered in the same gale off Cornwall.

Crew of the American brig *Edward* landing from the sea on the North Bull, in Dublin Bay, 1 December 1825. Drawn and lithographed by J.S. Templeton, working in London 1820-1845. Printed by Engleman.

There are the remnants of at least twelve wrecks on Portmarnock beach. One is probably the elusive *Jamaica Packet*, about which there is little information.

A beachcomber walking on Portmarnock beach describes beach movement revealing black sand where over the years he had found several gold rings and a sixteenth-century spoon. Six wrecks were visible at a low tide on 19 March 1999. Five were wooden, the sixth was metal. The wreck high on the beach has copper pins, indicating some antiquity and quality of building.

The *Bolivar* was wrecked on the Kish Bank during a snowstorm on 4 March 1947. During the war the newly built ship was sunk in a fjord in Norway. Refloated after the war, she was on her first voyage when lost.

The wreck of the *Bolivar* was dispersed by Irish Lights as a hazard to shipping.

Bolivar wreck notice.

The wreckage of the *Kilkenny*, which sank on 21 November 1991 after a collision with the *Hasselwerder*, was cut into three parts and raised onto the North Wall by the Smit Tak crane *Roland*. Three of the crew were lost.

The 763-ton Royal Mail Steamer *Armenian* was wrecked on the Arklow Bank on 24 February 1865. She was bound for Madeira and West Africa from Liverpool. The passengers were rescued by *Montague* but four crewmen from the Arklow light vessel were lost when their boat was upset in a rescue attempt.

A great storm wrecked shipping in Dun Laoghaire Harbour on 25 February 1933. The dredger *Fag a Ballach* broke loose and smashed boats against the pier. The *Cynthia*, a former liner tender at Lough Swilly, was then operating as a pleasure cruiser and was wrecked.

The 294-ton collier *Hampton* was driven ashore near Salthill railway station on 12 November 1901. She became a total loss.

The *Inveresk* went ashore at Sandycove on 12 November 1915. After a period ashore the vessel was refloated. The wreck was close to the Forty Foot bathing place and boys frequently swam to the wreck with terriers to attack the rats which had taken over the ship.

The *Fellinhelli* (75 tons), built at Dinorwic port and owned by Evans coal merchant in Greystones, the *Federation* and the *Reciprocity* were all driven ashore in October 1910 at Greystones harbour. All three were repaired at Arklow but *Fellinhelli* was lost on 25 January 1915 off Liverpool.

The 1,386-ton collier *Trifylia* was driven ashore at Newcastle, two miles south of Greystones, during the same gale as the *Inveresk* stranding on 12 November 1915. She carried coal from Ayr for Rouen.

THE ILLUSTRATED LONDON NEWS

No. 1883.—VOL. LXVII.   SATURDAY, SEPTEMBER 11, 1875.   TWO WHOLE SHEETS | SIXPENCE By Post, 6½d.

SINKING OF H.M.S. VANGUARD.—FROM A SKETCH BY ONE OF THE OFFICERS.

The reserve squadron of the Channel fleet consisting of five ironclads and the yacht Hawke left Kingstown for Cork. They encountered mist off Bray Head. The HMS *Vanguard* turned broadside to avoid collision with a sailing ship and was rammed by *HMS Iron Duke* which was next in line. The view of HMS *Vanguard* sinking on 1 September 1875, following the collision with the *Iron Duke*, is from a sketch by one of the officers.

THE ILLUSTRATED LONDON NEWS

No. 1885.—VOL. LXVII.   SATURDAY, SEPTEMBER 25, 1875.   WITH EXTRA SUPPLEMENT | SIXPENCE By Post, 6½d.

COURT-MARTIAL ON THE OFFICERS OF H.M.S. VANGUARD.

The court martial of the officers blamed the *Vanguard* for not trying to save the ship instead of ordering the crew to abandon immediately. There was no loss of life.

The wreck of *HMS Vanguard* as she appeared at high water.

Removing the yardarm from *HMS Vanguard*.

DIVING OPERATIONS AT THE WRECK OF THE VANGUARD.—SKETCHED FROM ON BOARD H.M.S. AMELIA DESPATCH-BOAT.

Diving operations at the wreck of *HMS Vanguard*.

The schooner *Agnes Craig*, owned by Kearon and Tyrell, was built by Ferguson and Baird at Connahs quay in 1884. She was bought into Arklow in 1912. In August 1952 she was broken and the hulk towed to sea and left to drift ashore at Arklow Rock. The *Agnes Craig* was among the last Arklow sailing schooners.

The *Asian Parade* ran ashore at 19 knots on the Codling Bank on 4 February 2000. The 55,000 ton vessel had landed 1,700 cars at Dublin and was en route to Rotterdam when she went off course and grounded like many earlier ships on the Codling Bank. The initial fear was that her oil tanks would rupture as the bank has many boulders. The oil was unloaded with some difficulty into a barge and initial efforts by three tugs failed to release her. At midnight on 6 February 2000 there was a high tide and she was freed and towed to Dublin Port for inspection. It was not a moment too soon, as by the afternoon a strong gale blew which would have damaged the vessel further.

The iron ship *Calcutta* was wrecked at Kilmore in Ballyteigue Bay on 17 January 1874. Data in the Board of Trade wreck register records that she was bound for Surinam from Liverpool. The legend at the back of the photograph suggests that she had loaded pyrites ore at Avoca and was wrecked in 1873.

The 451-ton Welsh coaster *Anna Toop* grounded in January 1958 on the bank south-east of Arklow. She carried sheet steel from Port Talbot to Derry. During refloating work in summer 1959 divers told the story that they found a submarine near the Arklow No.4 buoy.

Three
South East

The *St Austell* of Barnstaple was wrecked at Sandeel Bay, Fethard on 19 April 1952.

Figurehead of the American sailing ship, *Alfred D. Snow* which was wrecked off Waterford on 4 January 1888. The ship rounded the Hook and grounded abreast of Templetown Bay close to Bromhill shoals. The south-south-east wind quickly dismasted the ship and she went over on her side. The crew boarded their boats and remained attached by the painter. Meanwhile Captain Cotter of the tug *Dauntless* approached within half a mile of the wreck but could not get closer. The *Dunmore* lifeboat crew refused to launch though they would have had an easy approach from windward. The crew chose to drift to shore rather t han row out to the tug. Their boat was swamped in the surf and the crew of twenty-eight drowned. The *Alfred D. Snow* carried wheat from San Francisco to Liverpool. The 232-ft, 1987-ton ship was built in 1877 at S. Watts and owned by Watts.

The *Minorca*, stranded in January 1955 at Cahore beach, at the same place where 240-ton *Pioneer* was lost in 1914. The *Pioneer's* winch remains at the site and is uncovered at low tide. The *Minorca* was refloated by two Dutch tugs despite the captain's fears that she would be a total loss. A wicker basket which contained a stone jar of rum remains in the Strand Bar. Captain Van Der Mollen and his crew all survived.

The *Belfast harbour dredger No2* was on tow to Cork for scrapping when the tow parted. The vessel was washed ashore on 17 February 1966 at Orphan Girl beach, Ballymoney. The beach name refers to the loss of the schooner *Orphan Girl* there on 22 October 1881.

The *Mexico* was wrecked on the South Keeragh Island, Wexford on 20 February 1914. The Fethard lifeboat was also wrecked with the loss of eight of her crew, during the attempt to save the crew of the *Mexico*. Eight of the *Mexico* crew were saved by the five lifeboat survivors and all but one were rescued with great difficulty from the barren islet the next day by Rosslare lifeboat.

The *Manchester Market* owned by Manchester Liners was lost on the on the reef at Tuskar on 26 April 1903.

The *Crest* was wrecked at Rosslare on 1 March 1936. She carried a cargo of salt from Wexford to Dublin. She was owned by Mr Rochford of Kilmore.

The *Westgate* went aground near Passage East on 25 November 1998, due to a steering failure while outward bound. She was refloated by tugs and proceeded on her voyage.

The *Michael* was the last ship to be totally lost on Tramore beach and reputedly the first since the First World War. She went ashore on 14 January 1975. The wreck was dismantled on the beach.

The *Gladonia* proved that Tramore was still a significant danger to shipping when she went ashore in a gale on 13 January 1989. Her grain cargo was unloaded into trucks and excavators dug a channel. Then she was pulled off by the 5,000-ton tug, *Fair Play 9.*

The *Monmouthshire* was wrecked at Tramore on 11 January 1894. The 1,162-ton barque carried coal and machinery. (*Andrew Kelly Collection*)

The *Scott Harley* ran ashore at Tramore on 17 November 1894. The cargo of coal was removed into carts and the vessel eventually refloated.

The 300-ton French trawler *Fée des Ondes* was wrecked near Ardmore Head on 27 October 1963.

The 2,166 ton-steel barque *Marechal de Noailles* was wrecked just 200 yards west of Mine Head lighthouse on 14 January 1913. The crew of twenty-four were rescued by breeches buoy. She carried coal from Glasgow for New Caledonia. The *Hamburg* which stranded in Dublin Bay was her sister ship, formerly known as the *Marechal de Castro*.

Rescued Crew of the
Marechal de Noaills
Wrecked at Mine Head
On 16th 1913

Morgan

The 900 ton-coaster *Croghan*, commanded by Captain Kearns of Arklow, struck the rocks at the Hook on 1 March 1973. The vessel was badly holed and abandoned. On 20 March 1973 the *Croghan* was refloated by Mr Doyle of Coolbarrow, but the pumps were inadequate and she went down 100 yards off shore with the loss of one of the salvors.

The *Sea Fisher* went ashore at Waterford on 18 April 1912, but despite her precarious position she was refloated.

Matrisha at Bunmahon on 31 October 1991. An Alouette helicopter of the Irish Army Air Corps is assisting two of the crew to reboard the vessel and assess damage. The crew had been saved by an RAF Sea King helicopter. A month later the ship was refloated by the Irish Lights tender *Gray Seal* and the tug *Alma*.

The coaster *Willy* went ashore at Swines Head, Dunmore on 24 August 1999. She was refloated with the assistance of the tug *Port Lairge*.

The 1,200-ton Italian barque *Hansa* was wrecked in November 1899. She struck the ground outside Credan Head and came ashore between Credan and Western Bay. After being towed off she took ground again on the bar, but refloated during a storm and went onto Drumroe bank a mile and a half below Passage. She had sailed from New Brunswick with timber for Waterford.

The *Pembroke* went aground on the Little Saltee in February 1899.

A gun at Kilmore Quay which was raised by a trawler. Local folklore would have it that the gun came from a submarine, but it bears a French inscription on the base 'St a Ce MLS 1887 no 686-300 Kg pour CTR de 47' and on the gun 'CTR de 47 T50-5-1895 No 519 poids 132.' The ship from which the gun came must be French but no such wreck is known.

The *Eliza O'Keefe* was lost at Wises Point, Ballinacourty, Dungarvan on 15 February 1900. She carried coal from Newport for Dungarvan.

The *Nina Mendl* went ashore at the Furo on the Siur.

The *Cirilo Amoros* was wrecked at Gull Island between Stradbally and Ballyvooney on 15 February 1926. She was en route from Spain to Liverpool with oranges and rice. The local people, led by William O'Brien and Jack O'Keefe, plucked a lifebuoy with a line from the sea and established a rope to the shore. The crew then came ashore on a breeches buoy.

The remains of *Cirilo Amoros*, broken by seas and partially dismantled. Some traces remain to this day and are visible at low tide.

A local hooker came to grief on the wreck of the *Moresby* but was refloated. The ribs of the *Moresby* are still visible at low water.

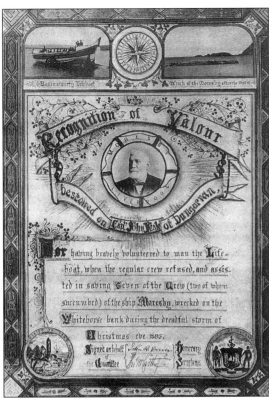

Certificates were presented to the scratch crew from Dungarvan who manned the lifeboat in an attempt to rescue the *Moresby* crew.

The *Peri* was lost at Seaview near Ring on 2 November 1907. She was owned by Moloneys of Dungarvan. Two of the crew of four were lost.

Hilda, 1898 wrecked at Duncannon.

The *Teaser* was wrecked at Curragh, Ardmore, on 18 March 1911. All aboard were lost. She was owned at Connas quay by Mr Ferguson.

The *Tyne* of North Shields ashore at Ballinacourty, Dungarvan in 1909.

The Dunmore East trawler *Jenalisa* sank without warning 2.5 miles off her home port on 5 February 1996. Though the vessel was raised by Celtic Salvage and Towing, no explanation was found for the loss of the vessel and her three crew.

Four
Cork

The 82-ton steam collier *Rover* of Cardiff went ashore at Whiting Bay, Youghal on 7 July 1899. The collier was badly damaged on her bottom. (*Jacob Collection at Waterford City Library*)

On 14 January 1996 the *Tonfield* was wrecked at Roches Point. The crew were rescued by helicopter. The wreck was removed in April.

On 10 October 1928 the *Celtic* went ashore at Roches Point. The 20,000-ton liner was one of four sisters; the others were *Cedric*, *Baltic* and *Adriatic*. They were built by Harland and Wolffe between 1899 and 1901. The sisters were the largest liners of their time. Salvage work by Cox & Danks continued for a year, but she was wrecked in a storm on 10 October 1929 just before she was to have been refloated. The only casualties were twenty salvage workers who were gassed by hydrogen sulphide fumes from rotting grain being removed. Four of them died.

The Dominion liner *Merrion* grounded at Roches Point on 2 March 1903. Tugs failed to refloat her initially, but after removal of cargo three tugs managed to release the stricken ship.

The paddle steamer *Vanguard* was wrecked on 28 December 1844 near Cork lighthouse. All aboard, including their horses and carriages, were saved by the *Ocean*, which came out from Cobh.

The *Irish Plane* was wrecked at Ballycotton on 1 February 1947. Formerly the *Arena* she was built in 1917 at Spooters Isle, New York. She was purchased by Irish Shipping in 1941 to bring essential supplies to Ireland during the war.

On 22 October 1928 the *Alison* was sunk in a collision with the collier *Zillah*, owned by Zillah Shipping and Carrying Co. Ltd. The wreck of the *Alison* was raised by Palmer of Ringaskiddy. They used two liner tenders as lifting vessels to raise and beach the *Alison*.

WRECK OF THE ASSAYE, EAST INDIAMAN, ON THE SOUTH COAST OF IRELAND.—SEE NEXT PAGE.

The *Assaye* went aground on 28 January 1865 in Ross Bay near Galley Head during fog. The ship was built as a paddle frigate in Bombay for the East India Company in 1854. The captain was drowned as he tried to swim ashore with a line, the remaining forty-eight were saved by a line fired from the shore.

Captain Arbuthnott's ketch, *Three Brothers of Rye*, broke her mooring and was washed ashore on the beach near the railway station at Youghal in 1961.

The 1,274-ton *Carnavonshire* was wrecked at Yokane Point near Lough Ine on 11 April 1896. She was en route from San Francisco to Queenstown for orders with a cargo of wheat. Built in 1876, she was owned by Hughes of Liverpool.

The 2,419-ton *Oswestry* was wrecked at Mizen Head, Co. Cork, on 12 March 1899. She carried cotton, copper and iron from Virginia, bound for Manchester. The crew scaled the cliffs to safety. Boats were organised by Mr Swanton, the Lloyds agent, to salvage the cargo.

The 4,500-ton, *Ailsawald* went ashore at Sherkin Island on 19 December 1900. She was en route from Penarth to Bermuda with 600 tons of coal as ballast when she was caught by wind and driven ashore. A storm drove her higher on the rocks.

The *Ailsawald* was towed into Baltimore and beached with her bow on Whitehall Level, but her stern was under twenty-three feet of water. A coffer dam was built on the deck and sealed. This allowed the water to be pumped out.

The *Ghazee* was torpedoed off Galley Head on 4 February 1917 and beached at Garretstown strand. Some of the vessel remains there to this day, breaking the surface at low water. Ships when torpedoed had orders to make full speed for the nearest beach, where they could be run ashore and salvaged if possible. This is probably why the *Lusitania* maintained speed, preventing the successful launch of most of the lifeboats.

The Guion line *Chicago* was wrecked on Chicago Knoll near Roches Point lighthouse during fog on 12 January 1868. She was built by Palmer at Jarrow in 1856. The 130 aboard and £60,000 in specie were unloaded without loss from the ship which was stranded on a reef 200 yards from the shore. The order of disembarkation was strict: female cabin passengers first, then female steerage passengers, lastly males then firemen and crew. Marines were called to guard the cargo and a looter was shot and wounded when he refused to leave a bale of cotton washed ashore.

The Ballycotton lifeboat rescued the crew of eleven from the *Alarm* of Belfast on 7 April 1886 at Ballycotton.

On 5 August 1898 the *Ecclefechan* ran ashore during fog inside Bird Island in Dunworley Bay. She was towed off by a team of tugs, beached and repaired by the Collins brothers, divers. The Ensor tog *Adelaide* is alongside.

The Inman liner *City of Chicago* struck the shore at the old head of Kinsale in fog on 22 June 1892. Her engines were kept at slow ahead to retain the ship from slipping into deeper water. *Bill Swanton*

The damage to the *City of Chicago* was severe. Despite the efforts of Captain Redfearn of the Liverpool and Glasgow Salvage Association she broke up quickly during a gale. (*Photo for Ensor via Bill Swanton*)

Celtic being dismantled. Palmer's ship *Shark* alongside.

The *Albion* was wrecked at Garretstown strand. The print is from the Peabody Museum, Salem Mass, illustrated from the memory of a survivor named Everport.

The *Tadorna* was wrecked on 15 November 1911 at Ballycrenane strand, east of Ballycotton. She had only been built in 1910 at Swan Hunter on Tyneside. She had driven over a reef and although she appeared intact and spectators could clamber aboard, she was a total wreck and broke in tow within days.

The *Dina* sank off Fastnet on 14 March 1994. She got into difficulties when diamond pressing machinery shifted, causing the vessel to list. The machinery was destined for De Beers synthetic diamond factory at Shannon.

The wreck of the *Killarney*, 26 January 1838 at Rennie Bay, Cork. Lithograph by John Brandard after a drawing by William Joy. The rescue of the passengers of the *Killarney* was a celebrated event and several sketches were published. One of the survivors, Baron Spolasco, wrote an account of the disaster and toured the country lecturing on the event.

A correct lithographic view of Renny Bay showing the rock on which the *Killarney* was wrecked with the survivors on it. Drawn and illustrated by Unkles, 26 South Mall, Cork, 'from a sketch taken on the spot' The rescue of the passengers after a prolonged ordeal was quite a feat of engineering and seamanship by a Mr Hughes.

The 703-ton paddle steamer *Sirius* was wrecked at Ballycotton on 16 January 1847. She had been the first steam ship to cross the Atlantic, arriving in New York f rom London on 23 April 1838, beating her rival the *Great Western* by just a few hours.

The carved dog figurehead from the *Sirius* is in Hull Maritime Museum.

A drive shaft from the *Sirius* was cut in sections to make commemorative medals by Masons of Birmingham, who salvaged the metal from the wreck in 1898. Another *Sirius* drive shaft was used at a spade mill for some years after salvage and was recovered and mounted at Passage West.

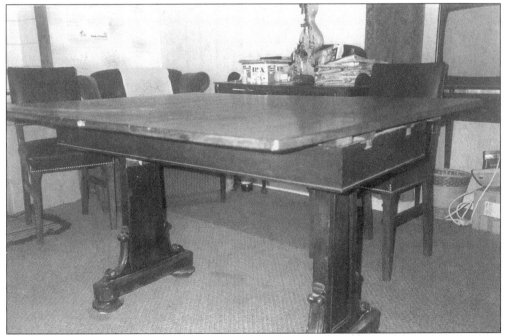

The table from the *Sirius* was recovered and made its way to Daniel O'Connell's house at Derrynane.

The 2,026-ton *Falls of Garry* was wrecked at Ballymaccus Point near Kinsale on 22 April 1911. The *Falls of Garry* had been refloated from a reef at Ichino in New Caledonia where she had been abandoned and sold for £47. She was then purchased by Copen, Craig & Walker of Glasgow and was en route to the new owners. On the voyage she had run out of food and been resupplied by HMS *Adventure*.

On 22 November 1986 the iron ore carrier *Kowloon Bridge* became the largest wreck in the world when she ran onto the Stags Rocks. The *Derbyshire*, lost with all hands during a typhoon in the China Sea, was a sister ship. There was controversy about the strength of structural members and speculation that the ships were not sufficiently strong to survive stresses imposed in rough seas.

The length of the deck of *Kowloon Bridge* gives an impression of the size of the vessel.

Ammunition at the *Aud* wreck site. The *Libau*, disguised as the neutral *Aud*, was scuttled at the entrance to Cork Harbour on 22 April 1916. She carried guns and ammunition from Germany for the 1916 Rising. The ship was intercepted off Tralee and escorted to Cork. The crew picked the location for scuttling carefully and thought they could block the harbour entrance.

The 5,242-ton *Berwindale* was torpedoed and captured on 16 March 1916 about thirty miles west of Fastnet Rock. The submarine was driven off. The ship was taken to shore at Bantry where she sank, a patch was fitted and she was refloated and taken to Liverpool. The cargo of 3,000 of wheat was pumped over the side as there were no buyers for the damaged goods.

The *Betelgeuse* wreck was removed by Smit Tak in an operation which lasted about eighteen months.

Five

West

The *Ranga* was wrecked at Slea Head near Dingle in March 1982. She was on her maiden voyage from Reykjavik when she lost engine power. The crew of fifteen were saved by RAF helicopter. In summer 1991 the bulk of the wreck was removed to facilitate filming work.

The *Port Yarrock* was wrecked at Kilcummin strand, Brandon Bay, on 29 January 1894 The 2,175-ton barque owned by Robert Rowatt of Glasgow, sailed from Santa Rosalia with a cargo of copper. The ship was in a bad way when she reached Tralee Bay, bu the captain refused to engage a local tug, preferring to await a Liverpool tug. The vessel was wrecked before the tow commenced.

Part of the *Port Yarrock* remains visible today. Two divers are laying a wreath on the occasion of the 100th anniversary of the loss. 2,200 tons of copper ore were salvaged by Moncas of Rosslare and Ensor of Queenstown over a period of twenty years.

Port Yarrock memorial at Killiney church. Captain Forbes and the twenty-two crew were all lost. The crew had been sick with scurvy throughout the voyage. The court of enquiry discovered that fifteen cases of lime juice had been loaded, but had been sold by the cook who committed suicide during the voyage. Most of the crew wrote letters from Brandon Bay which were posted by the captain the day before the vessel was lost.

On 4 December 1906 the 1,900-ton barque *Morven* was wrecked between Horse Island and Kilbaha in the Shannon. She carried 3,550 tons of wheat for Ballantynes of Limerick. The crew escaped by climbing the bowsprit.

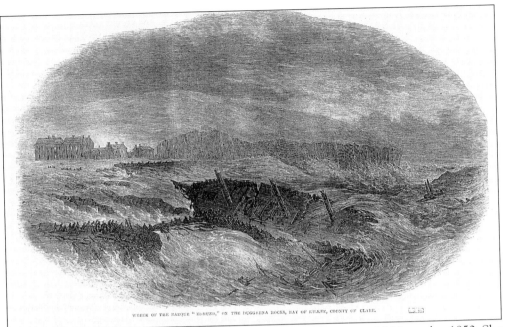

WRECK OF THE BARQUE "EDMUND," ON THE DUGGERNA ROCKS, BAY OF KILKEE, COUNTY OF CLARE.

The emigrant barque *Edmund* left Carraigaholt bound for America on 18 November 1850. She was blown back by a gale and wrecked at Kilkee. When the mast was cut it formed a bridge to shore and 111 were saved but ninety-six were lost.

The French sailing ship, *Léon XIII* was wrecked at Sarsfield point near Quilty on 1 October 1907. She carried wheat for Limerick. Local fishermen braved a terrible storm to take off some of the crewmen. The cruiser HMS *Arrogant* took off ten men.

The construction of the French Church at Quilty was aided by French subscriptions in gratitude for the rescue of the crew of the *Léon XIII*.

The bell of the *Léon XIII* still rings during Mass at the French church.

The *Elizabeth McLea*, an Arklow brigantine, was wrecked at Liscannor on 18 December 1894. She carried a cargo of Luagh stone. In February 1998 the wreck was uncovered at low tide and the cargo salvaged.

In March 1960 the *Plassy*, owned by the Limerick Steamship Company, went ashore in a hurricane on the tip of Inisheer, near the lighthouse. The wreck lies high and dry on the rocks. It is incredible that she should have been thrown so high, but the combination of a high tide, onshore wind and low barometric pressure raised sea level to an unusual height. The crew were rescued by rocket-thrown lines.

The 2,400-ton fish factory ship *Capitane Plevin II* went aground at Illaunloo rocks in Galway Bay on 5 April 1991. Despite fears that she would break up she was refloated by the salvage ship *Salvageman* about three weeks later.

The steam trawler *Nogi* went ashore at Straw Island in Galway Bay on 16 August 1938. She survived and was used as a minesweeper until lost on 23 June 1941.

Figurehead of a Spanish galleon wrecked at Streedagh in 1588. It was in the possession of Simon Cullen, Sligo, in the 1890s but the present location is unknown.

Diamantis Pateras was lost entering Sligo harbour on 23 February 1925. The ship grounded in a snow storm and broke her back as the tide ebbed.

The motor vessel *Greenhaven* was wrecked at Roaninis, Co. Donegal on 3 March 1956. A Westland Dragonfly from RNAS Eglinton suffered engine failure just after take off during the operation to rescue the crew of the *Greenhaven*. This was the first helicopter rescue in Ireland. Helicopter rescue was in its infancy and there were only a handful of earlier rescues. During the Korean war a pilot was rescued after ditching from an aircraft carrier. In December 1952 four crew were rescued from the Scrobie sands off Great Yarmouth. A USAF helicopter from Manston rescued the sole survivor from the South Goodwin lightship, lost during the great storm of November 1954. On 3 February 1956 forty-one men were saved from a ship in the Pentland Firth by helicopters from Lossiemouth.

The *Barrister* was wrecked on a reef off Inishark.

WRECK OF H.M.S. WASP AT TORY ISLAND, DONEGAL.—FROM SKETCHES AND INFORMATION SUPPLIED BY THE SURVIVORS.

The gunboat HMS *Wasp* was wrecked under the lighthouse at Tory on 22 September 1884. The commander Lt Nicholls and fifty of fifty-eight crew were lost. The gunboat was en route to the island with marines to enforce rent collection. Her propeller was raised and lies at the Maritime Museum at Greencastle.

The *Wheatplain* was wrecked at Tory on 27 March 1930. She carried 420 tons of flour for Spillers, of which 50 tons was saved by the islanders.

Salauat Yulayev ashore. She was refloated by Celtic Salvage and Towing.

Armada chest at Christchurch, Dublin. Such chest are reputed to have been washed ashore from the Armada. There is another explanation that these were used as collection boxes to gather money towards the welfare of soldiers. Though such coffers are referred to as armada chests they were the strong boxes of the sixteenth and seventeenth centuries. The particular Chatham chest was constructed in 1625 to hold the 'chest at Chatham'. This fund or chest was established by the treasurer of the Navy, Sir John Hawkins, in 1590 to provide pensions for sailors in poor circumstances after the defeat of the Armada. However, some are without doubt authentic Spanish items of the period. In Ireland these chest were in use at the time of the O'Donnells and probably came from trading between Donegal and the continent. The lid of this chest was dug up at O'Cleary's Castle at Kilbarron, Ballyshannon. A chest found in Mayo could be authentic because it was supposed to have been taken from the sea at Blacksod and bears corrosion appropriate to sea water. Cuellar's narrative mentions the Irish breaking open money chests from Spanish arcas at Stereedagh. These were iron chests with flat lids to hold money. The State Papers of 1588 have several references to money chests in Spanish ships.

Six
Wartime

The *El Zorro* was torpedoed on 28 December 1915 off the old Head of Kinsale. A tow was commenced but she was washed ashore at Man O War Cove near Cork. She was broken on the shore. Torpedoed ships were ordered to make full speed for the nearest beach. This tactic allowed some twenty ships to be salvaged with minimum fuss from sandy bottoms on the Cork coast.

It was presumed that UC 44 had been blown up by one of her own mines, but afterwards it was discovered that a clever ruse concocted by Admiral Hall, head of Admiralty Intelligence based at 'Room 40', had set a trap for the submarine. Normally, once mine laying had been discovered, the mines would be swept at the first opportunity. However, in this case the mines were left in position and UC 44 ran into the field lain by her predecessor.

UC 44 raised between camels. The intelligence gathered from UC 44 revealed the methods of the German submariners. The whole operation was extremely hazardous – not only did the submarine contain live mines, but the area had to be swept before the salvage could commence. During the sweeping the minesweeper George Milbourn was lost, on 12 July 1917.

UC 44 begins to be lifted. The submarine was lifted between two pontoons or 'camels' using the tide and limited winching. The lifting barges had tanks which could be pumped out to lift a submerged vessel some five feet off the sea bottom. Then the assembly was towed towards shore until it beached at low water. The tow recommenced at high water until the submarine was ashore.

Mine with its launching frame and anchor being removed from the wreck of UC 44.

THE SPHERE

AN ILLUSTRATED NEWSPAPER FOR THE HOME

Volume LXI. No. 799. London, May 15, 1915. Price Sixpence.

Some of the boats attempting to push away from the starboard side of the *Lusitania* when she was beginning to heel over at a steep angle. The list developed suddenly, endangering the boats which had just been launched on the starboard side. From a picture drawn with the assistance of eye-witnesses for the *Sphere*

The *Lusitania* was torpedoed and sunk on 7 May 1915 off the old Head of Kinsale. This was the worst shipping disaster on the Irish coast. Some 1,200 lives were lost.

An expedition to the *Lusitania*, seventy metres underwater, by Oceaneering in 1985 recovered many items, including the propeller now at Merseyside Maritime Museum.

The last plunge.

6.

e *Lusitania* loss has attracted many artists representations and souvenirs. The sinking of the
sitania became such a propaganda issue that some harboured the suspicion that Churchill had
gineered the loss to encourage the United States into the war.

NEW QUADRUPLE TURBINE   R.M.S. "LUSITANIA"   32,500 TONS, 68,000 HORSE POWER

e *Lusitania* and her sister the *Mauretania* were built with government subsidies and designed
be converted to armed merchant cruisers at the outbreak of war. Equipment was fitted to
w installation of twelve six-inch guns. However, the guns were not mounted. The cargo on
itania's last crossing included cartridges, explosives and shells.

A commemorative 'Kitchener' spoon intended for presentation to the *Lusitania* first class passengers and a fuse from a six inch shell from the late Ernie Greene's collection. This is proof that *Lusitania* carried live explosives. Ernie dived for Oceaneering on the mission to raise the propellers. A mailbag is in Kinsale museum, and two oars are in the church at Castletownsend. Many items are in the possession of the owner, Mr Bemis.

John Light and his crew dived the *Lusitania* breathing on air. This was remarkable given the depth involved, as at oxygen partial pressures of about 1.6 a diver is severe danger of unconsciousness from oxygen toxicity. The team operated out of Kinsale aboard the *Kinvara* between 1960 and 1969.

The cruiser HMS *Juno* was ordered to return to Queenstown lest it become a target, and the Kinsale fishing fleet took time to reach the stricken *Lusitania*. A Manx fishing lugger, the *Wanderer*, was first on the scene.

Mass funerals took place at Queenstown to the cemetery two miles outside the town.

Many photos taken at the time were for propaganda purposes. Contrast the real lifeboats below with the one with 'Cunard' written on the side.

The 'Cunard' boat was used in photos with apparently dead children. Many children lost their lives on the *Lusitania*.

The Admiralty trawler *Metres* was repaired at Liffey Dockyard during the First World War. She is believed to be the vessel which collided with and sank the *Guide Me II*.

The anti submarine drifter *Guide Me II* was sunk by a collision with one of her sisters on 29 August 1918. At the outbreak of war hundreds of fishing vessels were converted to sweep mines and manage anti submarine nets. The gun from the *Guide Me II* was raised and deposited in the Maritime Museum in Dublin.

The first torpedo from *UB 123* struck *Leinster* in the post room, killing all but one mail sorter who had gone on deck for a smoke.

During the First World War a patrol of airships was maintained at Malahide Castle. One of these was supposed to have accompanied the Leinster on her journey to Holyhead. However she was damaged in a gale and no anti-submarine patrol went out that day.

The mailboat *Leinster* sank on 10 October 1918 after being torpedoed. Just over 500 people were lost from the 700 aboard. The loss of life was the worst in any shipwreck in the Irish Sea.

A memorial with one of the anchors was erected in 1998 through the efforts of the owner of the wreck, Mr Des Brannigan. This is near the mailboat pier at Dun Laoghaire from where the *Leinster* sailed.

The 14,950 ton armed merchant cruiser *Laurentic* was sunk by a mine on 23 January 1917 just an hour after leaving HMS *Hecla*, the base ship, at Buncrana. Of the crew, 130 were saved but 350 died of exposure. Some £5 million in gold was recovered by Commander Damant and his men working from HMS *Racer* between 1917 and 1926. Commander Malet tried to recover the twenty-five missing gold bars in 1935. Then in 1985 Consortium Recovery worked on the wreck recovering many brass items. They also lifted this six-inch gun which lies in the Merseyside Maritime Museum. An armed merchant cruiser could often outgun a regular cruiser though an AMC had little armour.

The *Empress of Britain* caught fire after an attack by an FW Condor aircraft on 28 October 1940. The following day she was torpedoed and sunk. During salvage attempts in 1998 a skeleton was found in the gold storage section in the bow. It is believed that he was trapped when the ship sank while working on salvaging the gold cargo. The *Empress of Britain*, at 40,000 tons, was the third largest liner in the British Merchant Fleet.

Not all wartime wrecks are associated with the two world wars. Between 1796 and 1798, there was intense French naval activity off the west coast of Ireland. An attempt was made to land an army at Bantry Bay in December 1796. The frigate *l'Impatiente* was wrecked at Mizen on 30 December 1796 and the *Surveillante* scuttled in Bantry Bay a few days before. Another expedition landed troops at Kilalla too late for the 1798 Rebellion. A British fleet intercepted the French and a naval battle was fought off the Rosses in Donegal, thereby capturing Wolfe Tone. The anchor mounted in Donegal Town was abandoned by the *Romaine* in Donegal Bay when the defeated French force retreated to Brest.

The Q ship *Farnborough* was towed into Berehaven in a sinking condition on 22 March 1916 after a battle with *U 83*. Disguised as the *Loderer*, she cruised the south coast. Captain Campbell allowed her to be torpedoed and a 'panic party' abandoned ship. The submarine surfaced and was surprised and sunk by the substantial naval crew left aboard to work the disguised armament. The Farnborough was later salvaged by Ensor & Co.

The Flower class sloop HMS *Mignonette* struck a mine and sank outside Sands Cove in Clonakilty on 17 March 1917. Her sister ship HMS *Alyssum,* pictured helping the survivors, was mined and sank the next day. The Di Silva photographs are believed to have been taken by the twelve year old Baroness Di Silva, who lived at Castletownsend during the First World War and had her chauffeur take her out around the sinking ships.

The soldiers lost on the Leister are buried at the military cemetery at Blackhorse Avenue in Dublin

The *Malmanger*, a Norwegian tanker, was torpedoed on 12 March 1917 off the Fastnet. The HMS *Zinna* towed her towards land, but she sank three miles off the Beacon at Baltimore. The photo shows the stern high in the air with the bow 150 feet below on the seabed. The crew were rescued by the sloops *Mignonette* and *Alyssum*, both sunk within a few days. The wreck is now owned by Aodh O'Donnell.

The new 23,000-ton battleship HMS *Audacious* was mined and sank off Lough Swilly on 27 October 1914. The loss was so significant that the matter was kept secret and the ship remained on the fleet list throughout the war.

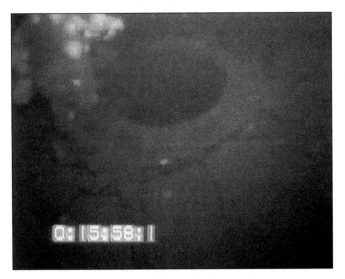

U 260 sank just off Union Hall on 13 March 1945. The crew had abandoned her following mine damage. The wreck lies at forty metres and this video view of the hatch was taken by the late Nic Gotto.

A metal box containing the *U 260*'s confidential papers was found floating by Mr Scully of Union Hall. It contained manuals, code books, maps and charts and three wheels marked Erasmus, Geheime Komando fache 2565. These may be the setting discs for the Enigma code machine.

At the end of the war in April 1945 the U-boats were ordered to surface off the coast. They were taken under guard to Lisahally in the River Foyle or Lough Ryan in Scotland.

After the removal of some essential equipment the U-Boats were then ballasted with concrete. Some sources say the concrete was used to embed anthrax and chemical warfare bombs being disposed of at the same time from the munitions complex at Faslane. Eighty-eight U-boats were taken to sea from Lisahally and scuttled during Operation Deadlight in November and December 1945.

Ammunition from the *Aud* on the seabed at the entrance to Cork Harbour. The *Libau*, disguised as the neutral *Aud*, attempted to land guns and ammunition from Germany at Fenit, Co. Kerry for the Easter Insurrection in 1916. The ship was intercepted and escorted to Cork where the crew scuttled the *Aud* off Roches Point on 23 April 1916 in an attempt to block Cork Harbour.

A standard patch shown on the *Alison*. The standard patch was made to fit almost any vessel by means of rubber gaskets. It invaluable in saving torpedoed ships during the First World War.

Seven

Gallant Rescue

Wrecked shipping in the harbour of Kingstown (now Dun Laoghaire) on the day of the Boyd rescue. While several ships were being wrecked outside the breakwater the scene inside the harbour was little better.

The rescue of the crew of the *Neptune* at Kingstown in 1861. The wall is merely seven feet high but assumes heroic proportions as illustrated, while the figures are reduced, for dramatic effect. Captain Boyd of the guardship *Ajax* was lost along with five of his men in the rescue attempt. There was only one survivor from the *Neptune*.

The Captain Boyd memorial at St Patrick's Cathedral. His grave is in the cathedral close.

Memorial to lost crewmen of the guardship *Ajax* at Dun Laoghaire pier, close to the spot where their rescue attempt ended so tragically.

The memorial at Carrickbrennan graveyard to the crewmen lost in the Neptune rescue attempt.

The *Palme* stranded off Seapoint in Dublin Bay during a storm on 24 December 1895. The Kingstown lifeboats put out to assist and the *Civil Service No.7* lifeboat was upset and all aboard were lost. The second Kingstown lifeboat, *Hannah Pickard*, was upset but self righted.

Upturned lifeboat *Civil Service No.7* on Merrion Strand, Dublin, 28 December 1895. It was assumed that the men were carrying a coffin but closer examination revealed that the man has a basket on his back, probably a cockle picker. The man in uniform is a coastguard, possibly from the guard party placed on the boat. The holes in the lifeboat were made in an effort to discover if there were any of the crew trapped underneath.

The nameboard of the *Palme* survives in the Maritime Museum at Dun Laoghaire. The frugal economy of shipowners at the time is demonstrated because when she changed name and owner the nameboard was turned. The back shows her former name, *Frederic Tudor*.

On 16 December 1917 the lighthouse tender *Tearaght* sank at moorings in Kingstown Harbour. She is being pumped out during salvage by the firm of Ensor. A coffer dam has been built on deck to exclude water. This was the *Tearaght* that eventually rescued the crew of the *Palme* some twenty years before.

A newly established helicopter service based at Waterford ended in disaster on its first day of official duty in August 1999, when the Irish Army Air Corps Dauphin crashed in fog at Tramore after a search and rescue mission. Captain Michael Baker, Sergeant Paddy Mooney and Corporal Niall Byrne died in the accident. This image shows the ill-fated Dauphin 206 on manoeuvres.

The use of rockets to carry lines out to vessels in distress was first envisaged by Congreve, whose rocket company fought in the American War of Independence and in the Napoleonic Wars. The system was perfected and Dennet's rockets were used by the coastguard. Each station in later years had a cart which contained the firing apparatus and ropes and lines of all sizes necessary to bring a crew ashore on a bosun's chair. An ingenious cutting apparatus was employed to sever the rope connected to the ship's mast after the last man was ashore. Rocket carts are preserved at Dun Laoghaire, Newbridge House and Valentia. This is the Greystones cart which was towed by a truck to Bray to rescue the crew of the *Marie Celine*, driven ashore in a south-easterly gale on 31 January 1921.

Eight
Salvage

The Daunt lightship *Puffin* was only eight weeks at anchor outside Cork Harbour when she was lost with all hands in a gale on 8 October 1896. The wreck was located by a team of divers working for Ensor's salvage company. The wreck was raised for the Irish Lights Commissioners to investigate the cause of the loss and whether the bow had been torn from the ship by her huge anchor.

During the civil war in summer 1922 there was heavy fighting around Cork between the Free State army and those who did not accept the Treaty. Troops were transported to Cork by sea in the *Lady Wicklow* and landed at Passage West. The channel upstream had been blocked by sinking the steamer *Gorilla* and the harbour dredger. Both were raised at the end of August by Ensor's salvage at a cost of £20,000.

McCausland divers at work. Strangford Lough and Portaferry were noted locations for salvage and ship dismantling. The firms associated with the work were McCauslands, Lees, Adams and Montgomery.

The *Fleswick* sank in Cork harbour on 17 October 1908 after a collision with the steamer *Killarney*. She carried 700 tons of coal from Garston for Suttons merchants. The wreck was raised by Ensor salvage company.

The firm of Palmer continued salvage work in the Cork area after Ensor's company was dissolved. They used their two liner tenders to raise the sunken *Alison*. The *Alison* sank after a collision with the *Emerald* on 22 November 1928. Palmer's vessel, *Shark*, assisted with Ensor's salvage of the *Silurus* and later in 1940 became a mine planter for the Irish Navy.

The row of houses known as Dollar Row was constructed at Whitstable by the Gann brothers as an investment after their successful salvage in 1834 of the silver dollars from the *Enterprise* on the Copeland Islands. The centre building is called Copeland House. The *Enterprise* was engaged in the notorious triangular trade from Liverpool when she sank en route to the west coast of Africa on 25 January 1803. The money was to buy slaves for the Caribbean plantations from which rum and sugar would return to Liverpool.

The Cork firm of Ensor worked to save the upturned dredger *Silurus* in Gareloch, Scotland after the First World War. They succeeded in an epic of engineering after a gigantic struggle. This crew would have worked throughout the First World War and saved some twenty vessels torpedoed off the south coast of Ireland.

Nine
Artefacts

Cannon from *Trinidad Valencera* being lifted into a temporary conservation tank in Donegal.

The table in Bunratty Castle is reputed to have come from a Spanish Armada vessel. It was formerly in Drumoland Castle. It is possibly from the *Annunciada* wrecked in the nearby Shannon.

Cannon from a Donegal Armada wreck.

This carronade lay outside the house of Daniel O'Connell at Derrynane, Co. Kerry. Its origin is unknown but in summer 1991 three cannon and two carronades were discovered underwater in the entrance to Derrynane Harbour. They appear to be commercial cannon from about 1790. There is no account of a lost vessel in the area.

The name of an inn on the coach road near Balbriggan is the Man o' War. The inn was established in 1585 and the pub was in situ in 1635. The origin of the name is unclear, although the sign is a carved head identified as that of a Turk or Magog, which may have been the figurehead of a ship wrecked nearby, perhaps at Mornington. The name Man o' War was in use as early as 1735. The Maxwell family preserved the head when they sold the pub.

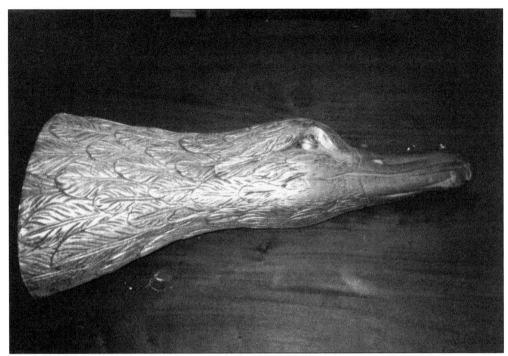

This Albatross figurehead was stored at Clontarf Yacht club. It was obtained by Paddy Farrell from a store at the coastguard cottages at Baldoyle prior to 1940, and is presumed to have come from one of the many wrecks in Dublin Bay.

'Shakespeare' a ship's figurehead washed ashore at Balliconigar, described as having come from the *Thames*, wrecked on the Blackwater Bank.

Lady in a green dress, the figurehead of the *Pomona*, an emigrant ship wrecked off Ballyconigar, Co. Wexford on 28 April 1859. Some 388 persons were lost but a whaler containing eighteen crew and three passengers reached safety. The *Pomona* was an American ship and was pressed into emigrant traffic because of the number seeking passage from Liverpool. After the *Pomona* disaster local merchants William Armstrong of Wexford, Mr Carty of Curracloe and Frank Hore of Wexford engaged divers. Jack Allen, an English diver, worked on the job of salvage for the Liverpool and Glasgow Salvage Association. Initially bodies were recovered and buried at St Mary's churchyard Wexford. Fear of plague from the decomposed bodies meant that no further burials were allowed at Wexford, and improvised burials occurred at Morriscastle, Ballyconnigar, Curracloe and Rosslare.

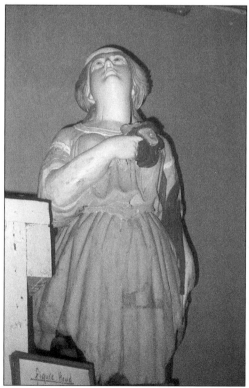

Figurehead from the *Test* of Harwich wrecked at Morris Castle on 15 January 1861. She was from Mauritius, bound for Glasgow with 450 tons of sugar. The figurehead is in the Wexford County Museum at Enniscorthy.

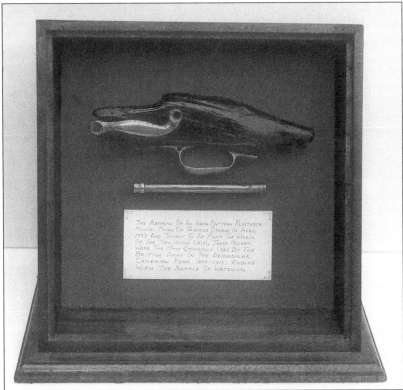

THE REMAINS OF AN INDIA PATTERN FLINTLOCK
MUSKET FOUND ON TRAMORE STRAND IN APRIL
1993 AND THOUGHT TO BE FROM THE WRECK
OF THE 'SEA HORSE' (1816). THESE MUSKETS
WERE THE MOST COMMONLY USED BY THE
BRITISH ARMY IN THE PENINSULAR
CAMPAIGN FROM 1809-1815. ENDING
WITH THE BATTLE OF WATERLOO.

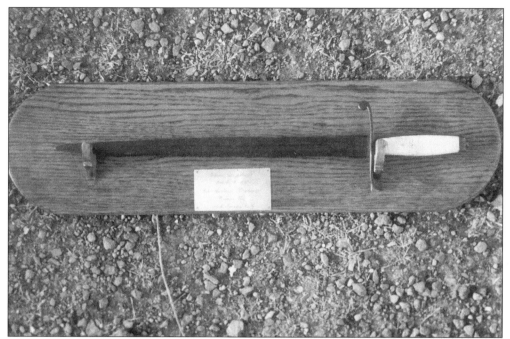

Above and previous page: The *Seahorse* was lost at Tramore on 30 January 1816. She sailed from Ramsgate for Cork carrying fifteen sailors, seventy-four women and 279 soldiers of the 2nd/59th Regiment The troops had recently returned from the Napoleonic wars in the Peninsula and the Continent. These were among the items from the washed ashore at Tramore. The Lord *Melville* and the *Boadecia* of the same convoy, were lost the same day near the Old Head of Kinsale.

Present and following page: Ship figureheads from unnamed Wexford wrecks in Wexford County Museum and in Kilmore Quay Maritime Museum.

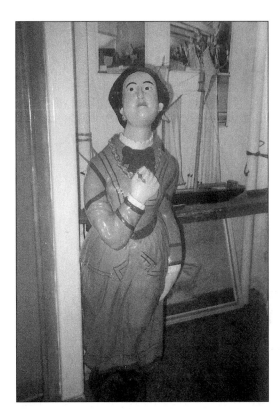

127

Acknowledgements

The author would like to express his grateful appreciation to the following whose pictures were reproduced or who otherwise facilitated the collection of photographs.
Military Archives, Cathal Brugha Barracks, Rathmines, Dublin 6; Commandant Laing for *U 260* memorabilia; Cormac Lowth and Roy Stokes for many photographs. Cobh Heritage Trust Ltd, for Ensor group of salvors; Derek Paine for Triflia and Greystones wrecks; Des Quigley of Dublin; Eoghan Cleare of Passage East for *Willy*; Andrew Kelly for Moresby, hooker at Morsbey site, Peri, and Rover; Stanley McKeown of Bangor for *Ulrica*, Pierce Hickey of Skibbereeen for *Kowloon Bridge*; The late Nic Gotto through Rachel Gotto for film of *U 260* and *Aud*; Patrick Shortall of New Ross; Lester Horgan; Strand Bar Cahore for *Minorca*; Riobard Mulcahy for *Port Yarrock*; Jacob Collection, Waterford City Library for several photos; Dave Donnan Collection; Mick Walsh of O'Shea's Bar Blackwater; Jim Blaney Collection for several photos; George Morisson, Gerald Lewis, Richard Palmer and the late Bill Swanton Collection for several photos; Jonathan Wigham and Maurice Wigham Collection; Irish Times for *Asian Parade*; Mick Crowley for *Lusitania* memorabilia; Illustrograph for the *Port Yarrock*; Gordon Campbell, *My Mystery Ships*; James Sherwood for *Cynthia* photo; Nicholas Tweedy of Fethard; Bernie Coakley of Waterford for several photos; Tony Caulfield of Tramore for *Matricia* and other photos; James Quain of Cork for *Marechaille de Noailles* photos; Dave Woosenam for Di Silva Collection; *Illustrated London News* for several photos; *Shipping Wonders of the World* for *UC 44* photos; Maxwell family for Man o War; Frank McMahon; Seamus Kirwin; Bernie Colclough of Waterford for several photos; Tony Caulfield for Tramore material; John Maddock for Crest; John Younge, Irish Army Air Corps; Celtic Salvage and Towing; Andrew Kelly Collection; Clare Champion; John Kelly. R. Kirwin of Limerick for *Diamantas Pateras*; Sea Breezes for HMS *Mystic*; Bernard Kaye for technical help. Many of the pictures were previously published in Shipwrecks of the Irish Coast Volumes One and Two by the author. I thank Cormac Lowth, Roy Stokes and Jim O'Dea especially for their patient proof reading and correction.

Further Reading:
Shipwrecks of the Irish Coast I, Edward J. Bourke, 1994, ISBN 0 952 30270 5
Shipwrecks of the Irish Coast II, Edward J. Bourke, 1998, ISBN 0 952 30271 3
Shipwrecks of the Irish Coast III, Edward J. Bourke, 1998, ISBN 0 952 30272 1
Shipwrecks of the Ulster Coast, Ian Wilson, 1989, Impact Coleraine, ISBN 0 9481 5405 5
Shipwrecks of the Donegal coast, Ian Wilson, 1999, Impact Coleraine, ISBN 09481 5456 X
Wreck and rescue on the East coast of Ireland, John de Courcey Ireland, Glendale, ISBN 0 9076 0609 1
The Harsh Winds of Rathlin, Tommy Cecil, Impact Coleraine, ISBN 0 9481 5465 9
A Gallant Barque, Sheila Mulcahy, The loss of the Port Yarrock, Brandon, 1999.
Lusitania, Patrick O'Sullivan, Collins 1998, ISBN 1 8982 5651 9
Death in the Irish Sea, Leinster, Roy Stokes, Collins, 1998, ISBN 1 8982 5652 7